Plants

Roots

Patricia Whitehouse

Heinemann Library
Chicago, Illinois

www.heinemannraintree.com
Visit our website to find out
more information about
Heinemann-Raintree books.

To order:
☎ Phone 888-454-2279
🖥 Visit www.heinemannraintree.com
to browse our catalog and order online.

©2009 Heinemann Library
an imprint of Capstone Global Library, LLC
Chicago, Illinois

Edited by Adrian Vigliano and Harriet Milles
Designed by Joanna Hinton Malivoire
Picture research by Elizabeth Alexander
Originated by Heinemann Library
Printed in China by South China Printing Company Ltd.

13 12 11 10 09
10 9 8 7 6 5 4 3 2

Library of Congress Cataloging-in-Publication Data
Whitehouse, Patricia, 1958-
   Roots / Patricia Whitehouse.
      p. cm. — (Plants)
Includes index.
Summary: A basic introduction to roots, covering their sizes,
shapes, and colors, as well as their function and uses to hu-
mans and other animals.
   ISBN 978 1 4109 3476 5 (HC), 978 1 4109 3481 9 (Pbk.)
   1. Roots (Botany)—Juvenile literature. [1. Roots (Botany) 2.
Plants.] I. Title. II. Plants (Des Plaines, Ill.)
   QK644 .W483 2002
   581.4'98—dc21
                  2001003653

Acknowledgments
The author and publishers are grateful to the following for
permission to reproduce copyright material: Alamy pp. **4** (©
Phil Degginger), **6** (© Marek Kasula), **11, 23** (© Grant Heilman
Photography), **12** (© Adrian Sherratt), **18** (© Caro); Corbis p. **9**
(© Alejandro Ernesto/epa); FLPA pp. **10, 23** (© Nigel Cattlin);
Gap Photos pp. **14** (Jonathan Buckley), 17 (Paul Debois); Getty
Images pp. **7** (George Grall/National Geographic), 21 (Daniel J
Cox/Stone); Photolibrary pp. **13** (J-C&D. Pratt/Photononstop),
16 (Andrea Jones/Fresh Food Images); Science Photo Library
pp. **8, 23** (Dr Jeremy Burgess); Shutterstock pp. **5** (© Malcolm
Romain), **15** (© Petr Jilek), **19** (© Monkey Business Images),
20 (© W. Woyke).

Cover photograph of buttress roots in a rainforest in northern
Queensland, Australia reproduced with permission of Photo-
library/Oxford Scientific (OSF)/Michael Fogden. Back cover
photograph of a cooked carrot reproduced with permission of
Shutterstock (© Monkey Business Images), and roots in soil,
Shutterstock (© Malcolm Romain).

We would like to thank Louise Spilsbury for her invaluable
help in the preparation of this book.

Every effort has been made to contact copyright holders of
any material reproduced in this book. Any omissions will
be rectified in subsequent printings if notice is given to the
publisher.

Contents

Some words are shown in bold, **like this**. You can find them in the Glossary on page 23.

What Are the Parts of a Plant?

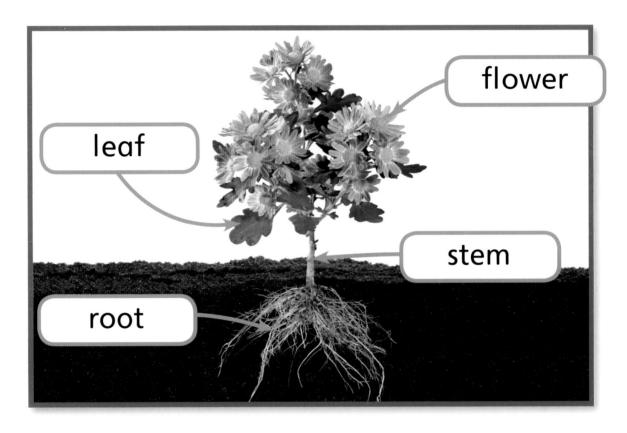

flower

leaf

stem

root

There are many different kinds of plants.

All plants are made up of the same parts.

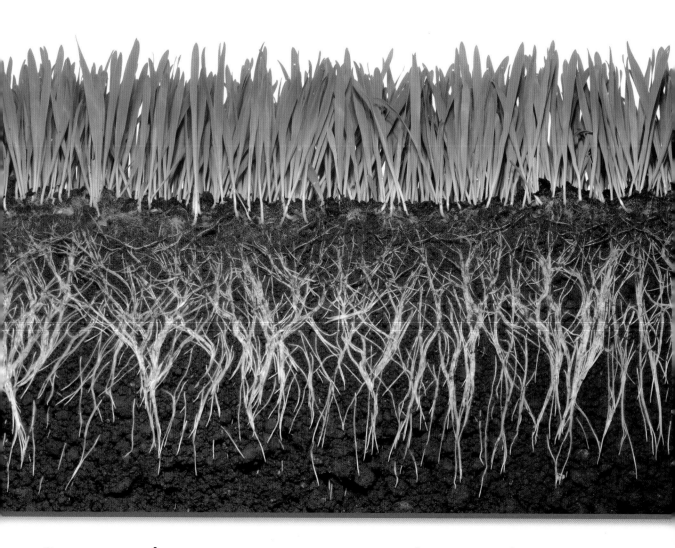

Some plant parts grow above the ground in the light.

Roots grow below the ground in the soil.

What Are Roots?

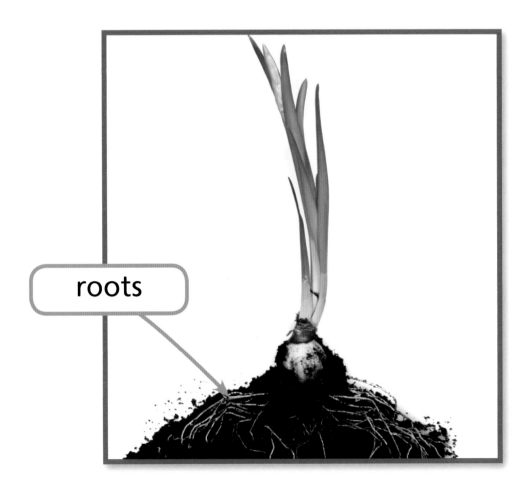

roots

Roots are plant parts that grow under the **stem**.

Some roots grow just below the ground.

Some roots grow very deep below the ground.

Water lily roots grow at the bottom of ponds and lakes.

Why Do Plants Have Roots?

root hairs

Plants need water to grow.

The **root hairs** soak up the water that plants need.

Roots also hold plants firmly in the ground.

Roots stop trees from being blown down by strong winds.

Where Do Roots Come From?

seed

root

Roots come from **seeds**.

The root is the first plant part that grows out of a seed.

leaf

stem

root

Roots grow downwards into the soil.

Then a stem grows upwards into the light.

How Big Are Roots?

Roots come in many sizes.

These leeks have roots that are short and thin.

Some roots are long.

Mangrove roots are long and thick.

How Many Roots Can a Plant Have?

Some plants have just one root.

Radish plants have one fat root.

Some plants have lots of roots.

This tree has hundreds of long roots.

What Color Are Roots?

Many plant roots are white, but roots come in different colors.

Beets and radish plants have red roots.

Carrot plants and sweet potatoes have orange roots.

How Do People Use Roots?

People use some roots for food.

We sometimes eat carrot roots raw.

Sometimes we cook roots before
we eat them.

How Do Animals Use Roots?

Animals use roots for food, too.

Guinea pigs have sharp teeth for biting into roots.

Some animals shelter among
tree roots.

They make their homes in roots.

Measure and Record

This bar chart compares the lengths of some different roots.

Can you see which plant has the longest root here?

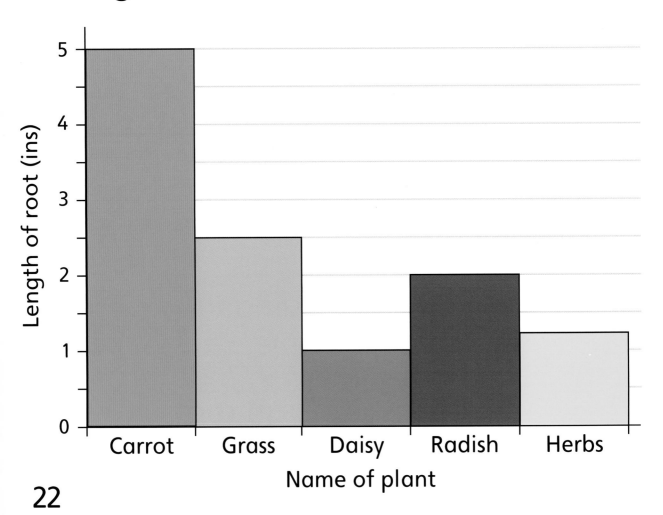

Glossary

 **root hairs** the parts of roots that are so small, they look like hair

 **seed** the part that new plants come from

 **stem** the part of a plant where the leaves and flowers grow

Index